# Lost on Purpose

# Lost on Purpose

Poems

Karen Head

Iris Press
Oak Ridge, Tennessee

Cover Photograph: "Handbag" by Colin Potts

Book Design: Robert B. Cumming, Jr.

Iris Press
www.irisbooks.com

Library of Congress Cataloging-in-Publication Data

Names: Head, Karen J., author.
Title: Lost on purpose : poems / Karen Head.
Description: Oak Ridge, Tennessee : Iris Press, [2019]
Identifiers: LCCN 2019007489 | ISBN 9781604542554 (pbk. : alk. paper)
Classification: LCC PS3608.E228 A6 2019 | DDC 811/.6—dc23
LC record available at https://lccn.loc.gov/2019007489

# Acknowledgements

*Atlanta Review:* "To the Roses of Auvillar"

*Blue Fifth Review:* "Settling Down" and "On Being the Only of My Circle Not to Watch *Twin Peaks*"

*Blue Five Notebook:* "When it doesn't rain"

*By the Light of a Neon Moon: Poetry Out of Dance Halls, Honky Tonks, Music Halls, and Clubs:* "Always Open"

*Gris-Gris: The Journal of Literature, Culture, and the Arts:* "The Other Side of the Tracks" and "Proximity"

*If You Can Hear This: Poems in Protest of an American Inauguration:* "Listen to Michelle Obama Denouncing Donald Trump's Abuse of Women"

*Mothers Always Write:* "Ask and Embla" and "Rifts"

*Nasty Women Poets: An Unapologetic Anthology of Subversive Verse:* "The Other Side of the Tracks"

*Loose Muse Anthology of New Writing by Women, Volume 1:* "Living in an Old Flower Shop"

*Loose Muse Anthology of New Writing by Women, Volume 2:* "Marriage Parable" and "Saltburn-by-the-Sea"

*Loose Muse Anthology of New Writing by Women, Volume 4:* "The Other Side of the Tracks" and "The Broken Mirror"

*One Trick Pony Review:* "Writing Poetry is a Luxury"

*Poets and Artists:* "Cleaning Out the Pantry," "Mapplethorpe: Early Polaroids."

*Poetry International.* "But for the Grace," "Flight," and "What We Missed"

*Starry Rhymes: 85 Years of Allen Ginsberg:* "In My Kitchen in Atlanta"

*The Connecticut River Review:* "New" and "Winogrand, Untitled"

*The Ekphrastic Review:* "The Reason for So Much *Love Poetry*" and "Derrière la gare de Saint-Lazare"

*The MacGuffin:* "Encountering Mary Outside Lourdes" and "Market Day"

*War, Literature, and the Arts:* "Crowning Glory" and "Sagittarius"

*Wild Musette:* "When Garden Gnomes Fall in Love"

Winner of the *2010 Oxford International Women's Poetry Prize:* "Three Moments."

Portions of this book were completed during three residencies at the Hambidge Center for the Creative Arts and Sciences and at the Virginia Center for the Creative Arts-France. I am grateful to have been selected as a fellow for these residencies.

Support for this book was provided by the Ivan Allen College of Liberal Arts and the School of Literature, Media, and Communication at the Georgia Institute of Technology. Thanks to my dean, Jacqueline Royster, and my chair, Richard Utz.

Thanks to my publishers at Iris Press, Bob Cumming and Beto Cumming.

My deepest gratitude to Liz Ahl, John Alexander, Ivy Alvarez, Grace Bauer, Brandy Blake, Julie Bloemeke, Gilbert Cockton, Cheryl Fortier, Randi Gunzenhäuser, the Hambitches, Marilyn Kallet, Ilya Kaminsky, Collin Kelley, Ted Kooser, Anne-Françoise LeLostec, Agnes Meadows, Sarah Oso, Linda and Bill Pratt, Thomas Ruehle, Carol Senf, Rosamund Stansfield, Bert Thornton, Bill Todd, Dan Veach, my friends, my family, and to the NDYPs (Blake Leland, JC Reilly, and Bob Wood) for reading, critiquing, or otherwise supporting this project. Y'all ROCK!

I am grateful to have a family who has always been part of my adventures. Mom, Dad, Mike, Maureen, Jason, Steef, Helen, Rose, Henry, Vic, Rose, Ruth, David, Karen, Dot, Dick, Mark, Harry, and Emma. I love you all.

# Contents

THE NEW WORLD

EPILOGUE

For Colin

# Prologue

# Residency

The man whose house overlooks the river
plays his accordion in the early evenings,
stands alone in his doorway, red bellows
opening and closing and opening
like labored breath then sigh then breath.
He plays for himself and for the air
and for the river and the rooster on the hill,
but he pays us no mind when we walk by,
not even if we stop and stare.
Whatever he is about, it has nothing
to do with us, just visiting artists—
a sculptor, a photographer, a poet—
he must dwell in the everyday realities
of this place, no time for reverie.

# UNITED KINGDOM

# Arriving at King's Cross Station

*What will survive of us is love.*
—Philip Larkin

The weekend in Yorkshire: you had taken me
Full of new love
Across the moors to meet your family.
Now, you shuffle the suitcases above
Waiting for me to find our place in his book—
To realize we're like Larkin's arrows
Shot from the same stone tunnel into sun-
Kissed rain. Windows fogged, we can only look
Forward to our own Whitsun fete. Time narrows,
Hearts pound. Even at our age this is fun.

## In the Photo We Look Like Characters
## in a Mike Leigh Film

We have come to Essex,
halfway between London
and the edge of Southend pier,
for a day-visit on summer holiday.
The garden is everything
it should be, without seeming so—
that hydrangea just happens
to grow next to that dwarf maple
ringed by candy-coloured impatiens.
Even your dead father's koi pond
has an air of the arbitrary
despite your step-mum's obsessive tending,
simply a tribute to him, she says.
Even the weather is uncannily good,
although a little cool in the shade.
The chronicle of family news is banal.
It is easy to blame jet-lag,
as I lean back and let my eyes close.
The family dogs sleep in the sun.
Then the story slips in,
how your cousin's wife snapped,
threw something (the teapot?).
She was aiming at her husband, but
nearly struck their toddler.
We all sit up straighter, clear our throats,
avoid each other's eyes.

If this were a Leigh film, now is when
the oblivious bachelor vicar would appear,
flustered from some trivial catastrophe
on the motorway or at a council meeting,
full of apologies for arriving late.
Then the neighbor, the one who always
has a drink in her hand and wears a too short skirt
would wriggle through a side gate,
and begin flirting with him.
We would all act as if nothing was untoward—

exactly as we do in the moment the shutter snaps.

# Wales and Chastity

*What hath night to do with sleep?*
*Night hath better sweets to prove.*
—Milton, "Comus"

If the plan is to escape temptation,
the pastoral setting makes little sense
a place where language
is only partially familiar,
and no defense against desire.

The danger comes at night,
when misplaced vowels moan, chant,
lure you into riotous forests,
call you to ecstasy, compel you
to lose yourself in dance.

At daybreak, brothers will not find you
fixed magically to a chair, innocent
and in need of Sabrina's freedom song.
You will sigh in slumber, wrapped in silk,
wake to find the empty cup beside you.

## Saltburn-by-the-Sea

Along Marine Parade, across from the prom end
of the funicular railway, just where it dives to the pier,
she appears on a balcony, holding fast to one French door.

Her faded pink tulle skirt (princess? ballerina? fairy?)
is sprinkled with sequins, shimmering in mid-afternoon light.
Her hair is a tangle of dirty blonde seaweed.

She is singing. Loudly. But I cannot make out the tune.

The building is not one of the restored ones on this circus:
weather beaten, bits of plaster clumping like barnacles,
windows dark with age even the North Sea can't clean.

I wave to her. She backs into the shadows—a siren in training.

# Time Passages

### Greenwich

London to our backs,
we climb the steep hill,
(tourists on summer honeymoon)
the path crisscrossing the Meridian,
one moment we are east,
the next we are west—
when we reach the summit,
we wait, giddy like schoolchildren,
for our turn on the line
the classic photo-op,
when instinctively you step west,
tell me to stand on the east
because that is where we are from,
but just before the shutter snaps
I push my left pinky toe across the line,
because where I'm from
will not dictate where I am going.

### The Time Lady

Selling time has always been a commodity—
something Ruth Belville understood,
her family business spanned two centuries,
and like her father and mother before,
each Monday she climbed to the Royal Observatory,
set her chronometer (she called it Arnold),
and then, like Prometheus, would descend
into the London streets with a different fire,
a fixed element that eludes and consumes us.

## Time Lord

I want to be a real time lord,
not a BBC character,
more in sync with Harrison's horology,
be inducted, full privilege,
into the Worshipful Company of Clockmakers,
my delicate workings navigating the waves
that separate today and tomorrow,
(or is that today and yesterday?)
able to define the lines from pole to pole—
as subtle as the line between look and leap,
between what we know and what we believe.

# On Visiting Douglas Adams' Grave

*Highgate Cemetery, 2010*
*42 pens sprout in front of his marker*

Pens slip quietly through wormholes in space
to a planet where I absolutely want to live.

Every morning I could take a walk
in that writers' world,
jot plans in my daybook—

I might challenge my BIC from 3$^{rd}$ grade
to play cribbage,
cajole my high school purple Flair felt tip
to help me choose new wallpaper,
invite the Montblanc I lost in a divorce
for afternoon tea—

I'll ignore the steadfast ballpoint
always prompting me to do more
than wait for inspiration.

# Give Way

There is a photo of me,
tourist in harlequin print raincoat
fake-smiling at Westminster Abbey
oblivious to the traffic sign
between me and sanctuary
that reads, "Give Way,"
a warning I've tried
to ignore.

Understanding and believing
I can be this generous is consummate
surprise:
    Like when I was eleven,
and fell down a flight of stairs,
all breath knocked out of me,
my granny refusing my panic—
locking her eyes with mine
blowing her breath hard on my face
until I gasped, cried out
with joyous fright.

That's how it is, this love,
especially in the animal moments
when previous experience warns me
to look away or close my eyes,
keep the distance that will allow
for quick retreat.

Instead, my right palm is braced
against your shoulder, my thumb
strains toward your left temple,
and as I push back my hair
with my free hand, in the moment
just before I give way completely,
I become lucid, know why
I will never again look away.

# The Secret Garden

1957

When you are three,
all gardens seem secret,
magical, especially those
you can only peek into,
sneaking is another kind of secret—
like the walled garden
you can just glimpse
from the corner window
in your tiny bedroom,
where evenings, fighting sleep,
you climb atop an old
nursing chair, and, turtle-like,
extend your head into
the cooling, London air,
breathe in the scent of lilac,
listen for the 20:37 to whistle,
stay as still as possible.

# Aries

The moors can be stark even in late spring,
but this year the heather explosion
came early, an amethyst haze
like ground fog idling along the hillsides.

We turn a corner and find the road impassable,
a grazing sheep flock has escaped, nothing to do
but pull over on the narrow shoulder,
watch the sun rise and listen to Bach's *Fantasia*.

We decide to stretch our legs,
take a few photos, admire the view.
I round the back of the car and find myself
locked in a gaze with a scruffy ram.

My body tenses; he seems less unsettled,
bobs his head three times, snorts,
ambles off to nibble grass—
dumbfounded, I begin to breathe again.

## Pancake Day

You do not believe in God.
On Shrove Tuesday you are not
worried about penance for sins,
not contemplating any sacrifice.

You do believe in the pancake,
a vestige of your Church of England
upbringing, an unassuming
but extravagant tradition.

This devotion leads us, each year,
to a hot griddle, splayed with batter.
We coax the tiny bubbles,
watch vigilantly for fixed edges
patient as can be, until
we are ready for the flip.

It is always in the late evening
when we eat this thin testament
dripped with syrup.

# At the Albion Beatnik Bookstore

Oxford, 2011

Dennis has just insisted
I have a piece of week-old sponge cake,
(it'll go off any minute).
The strawberry filling is a little too red,
but I love his shop,
and as I take the first dry bite
I hear a young man, a student in literature,
(the Derrida a dead give-away)
say to an obviously smitten girl,
"All poets are whores."
The scent of bergamot in my tea
starts to soften my scowl,
and I notice Rossetti's *The House of Life*
wedged in the corner of the bottom shelf.
As I pull out the volume, I think,
"Really, all poets are thieves."

Dante, I cannot blame you for wanting
to repossess the poems, even if it meant
disturbing Lizzy in her Highgate grave.
You fed on her day and night
to fuel your own fantasies,
but wanting to take back your words
does not mean you loved her less—
it is not the muse's place to possess the art.
What I cannot forgive is your cowardice,
sending Charles to her grave.
It should have been you
who pulled the worm-fed leaves
from her tangled copper hair.

# The Forgotten Woman

after a painting of an unknown woman
in Gladstone's Library

In the early years, I resisted a little.
Still the mistress of myself,
I had not completely
mastered the art of anonymity.

I liked the painter, his soft green
eyes, his tiny ear-lobes,
his crooked left pinkie finger.
I saw him mornings in the orchard,
would tickle his whippet's muzzle
while he pocketed fruit for lunch.
We spoke little.

The day he commented on my new dress,
said how striking it would be in his composition,
*that day*, when no one else cared to notice,
I said yes and meant it for a change.

He never asked my name.

When I saw my likeness, framed,
about to drop that blossoming orange,
I felt I'd ventured too far.
I was not destined to be a woman of history.
Russet is no color for the forgotten.

In another life, I've become a silent girl,
the one who visits the gallery on open days,
the one who skitters away when the docent approaches,
the one who nicks a withered plum by the gate.

It isn't difficult to be a mystery—
to have people walk by each day
noticing, but not noticing you—
to be just another woman
no one can name.

# Compline

The last chant before the Great Silence
should be heretical (truth without restraint).
Before resignation you need
a prelude to tantalizing dreams—
your nights ordained for chastity.

When you are willing only
for a quick retreat,
eyes locked for a rushed side glance,
hands grasped merely in parting,
fingertips frozen by obedience,
the loss is not from absent act,
but from absent expression.

In morning the poet wakes,
wayward, impoverished spirit,
all prayers still unspoken
the desire for indulgence
manifest in mock aubade.

# Southend-on-Sea

*The Pier is Southend, Southend is the Pier.*
—John Betjeman

A ride on "John Betjeman"
isn't what you think—
where mud flats mark the edge of land,
tinny cars begin their rattle and clink

down Southend Pier for over a mile.
Here the Thames is like a sea.
His namesake train makes me smile,
with its kitschy poetry—

Near the Kursaal, we visit tourist shops:
tea towels and kiss-me-quick hats.
At the casino bar, the bells never stop.
Your beer, my cider, both a bit flat.

Sir John secretly approved, I suspect;
simple charms seduce even a laureate.

## When Garden Gnomes Fall in Love

She has taken to keeping the pigeons,
imagines, at least, they are doves,
almost remembers the color of his eyes.
Why must there always be a sacrifice?
Before he was toppled
their summer nights together, always warm
under the hawthorn beside the chapel
possessed a hint of harmony:
whatever their desires,
the elements or mischance
must end them.

# Lost on Purpose

In the office of lost property on Baker Street,
bins are filled with mobile phones constantly chiming and chirping.
A black velvet evening coat hangs on a beach chair,
its rhinestone buttons cast light fragments on the wall.
In one corner, an urn (half-filled with ashes, I'm told)
tops an overturned red enamel saucepan.
On the glass shelf behind the information desk,
a set of yellowed false teeth are poised to nip a marble Krishna.
There are snowshoes, Impressionist prints, a rocking horse,
a claw-foot tub overflows with books. I count seventeen garden
    gnomes.

I consider inquiring after the tiny, silver key
that opened the lacquered box I got for my eleventh birthday,
the shamrock brooch my granny gave me,
and my first amber ring—maybe they turned up here.
Perhaps I can reclaim long-lost friends, the years 1984-88,
my mother's memory. Suddenly I find myself
holding a wedding cake knife, and I shudder, goose-pimply,
when I notice the engraved "K."
Some things, I remember, are lost on purpose.

# Whitby

*"The seagulls sound maniacal," you warned.*
*"Summer mornings sleep is impossible,*
*even if it rains, and it usually does."*

Perhaps this is why Stoker,
landed Dracula here, soundtrack
echoing against the rocky cliffs,
waves from the North Sea slamming
thick mist across the town.
Twice a year the modern Goths arrive,
hair bleeding black or purple dye,
drape themselves across tombstones
in St. Mary's cemetery, cameras clicking.
New jet crosses hang loosely from their necks.
Where sea converges with moorland,
one can easily imagine, in Yorkshire fog,
the faint shapes of Hilda and Caedmon
walking together near the east cliff,
Streoneshalh Abbey still intact, not the shell
that Vikings, Henry VIII, the Kaiser's navy,
and time have made of it. The ruin casts shadows
where ravens perch, the flutter of wings
and cawing the only remaining music.
Midday, I climb the hundred ninety-nine
steps from the harbor,
cobblestones leading to nothing
more sinister than the smell
of smoked kippers and a little labored breath.

# Ask and Embla

*According to Norse mythology
the first humans were formed
out of two pieces of driftwood.*

Fifteen years ago, you pleaded for it—
this simple piece of driftwood art
sold by a neo-hippie rastaman peddling
out of the back of his van at Talland beach.

After a long day of swimming
while your mother brushed sand from your feet,
your blanket, your hair (sand was everywhere,
and maybe a speck or two still
made you squinty in the sunset),
it was the kind of thing any child would marvel at.
In the fading light, it really did look like a dove.

You've moved it from your childhood bedroom
to a dorm-room to the kitchen in your first flat.
Now it hangs over the changing table in the nursery.

This summer, you take your children, five and two,
to make their first sand-castles.
On blocks you see a familiar VW bus—*Can it be?*
The artist, a drifter who never drifted,
drinks a latte while he notes a sale on his laptop.
His beard still looks like tidewrack,
but his head has washed smooth,
like the back of the driftwood turtle
your daughter now cradles.

# The Shipwreck

If we believe Turner,
everything
hinges on the sublime—

the storm
rages,
the ship nearly

overwhelmed
but still
afloat

crests
the turbulent waves,
the people,

inconsequential,
in lifeboats,
under smoky clouds,

and the main sail
illuminated—
nothing but a trick of light.

# Ruminations on Vaughn Williams' *Tallis Fantasia*

This is no "cow staring over a fence,"
but if it were, it would not be
any cow, or any fence:
really a hedge, an unkempt opening
onto a rolling, verdant meadow,
and on the horizon, half the sun.
The cow, a gentle Jersey,
wide eyes like white-rimmed onyx,
placidly chews, her neck bell punctuates
birdsong and a gentle breeze—
and everywhere and nowhere,
there is joyful lamentation.

# Sagittarius

Leave behind the old myth of centaur
ready to launch his arrows,
and sing yourself back to childhood:

*I'm a little teapot,*
*short and stout,*
*here is my handle…*

Keep your eyes heavenward.
You can see the Milky Way,
steaming from the spout.

The English serve a cuppa
in response to anything, even war.
This constellation is about peace.

# CONTINENTAL

# Derrière la gare de Saint-Lazare

after Henri Cartier Bresson

It is the *just before*
of the moment
that captures
us and the man
suspended inches above
the unavoidable water—
too soon to know
if the impact will produce
only childlike splash
or soaked frustration before
a long train ride to Cherbourg,
his shadow still
a perfect reflection
the impending ripples
we know will reach
the edges of experience.

# Daily Commute

Barcelona

It is 7:43, and the sun hangs just at the tree line.
I have surfaced from Urgell station onto Gran Via,
the vibration of the metro train pulses under foot;
the coastal breeze pushes a hint of saltiness north.
After ten weeks, I have moved from tourist
to something of a regular—

The woman with the red, lace-trimed fan,
taps at a young man to give me the seat beside her
when I connect at Plaça d'Espanya for the L3,
and the local butcher only sighs now when I stutter
in Catalan: *Pollastre. Tallada en dues.*
Even if only requesting cut chicken, it is best to avoid Spanish.

My favorite part of the day arrives when I do,
at the intersection of Carrer de Casanova.
On the corner bench, four sit, one stands,
every day, these bald bastions of anti-Franco sentiment,
still cool enough to pause their daily debates,
to take notice of the American woman.
No words, in any language, ever pass between us.

# Three Moments

after Mina Loy

### I. One O'Clock at Night

*Though you have never possessed me*
*I have belonged to you since the beginning of time.*

When a woman dreams, she is caught
as much by past and future
as by the present.
She must account for all the times—
hers and hers and his and his and hers—
and all of those connections.
Someone or other possesses each of us,
even if they have never met us,
will never meet us, are simply
a force that wakes us
from dead sleep into dark morning.

### II. Café du Néant

*The woman*
*As usual*
*Is smiling     as bravely*
*As it is given to her to be*

It could be any nightclub
where the naïveté of the young girls
is apparent—they regard nothing more significant
than the decorations in their drinks,
umbrellas too tiny for any storm.
They are drinking too fast.
They pretend not to look at her,

the woman sitting at the corner table.
Her loneliness a horror
they find more repulsive than death.

### III. Magasins du Louvre

*All the virgin eyes in the world are made of glass*

All museums should provide free admission to prostitutes.
The art is never as interesting
as watching women who are trained
not to gaze. Here their eyes engage,
take in the light, the odd angle,
catch ambiguities most of us never see,
turn the critical eye other women are instructed to distrust
to visions of paradise that are unashamed.

# When it doesn't rain...

Caillebotte, *Le Pont de l'Europe*

she holds her own parasol,
has chosen ruffles, red feathers,
a younger man.

She does not take his arm—
lingers one-half step behind,
forces him to turn to her.

The spaniel will trot past.
It might try for a quick sniff.
It does not symbolize fidelity.

## The Reason for So Much *Love Poetry*

Not everything in life should make sense.
Eluard knew it. Magritte did, too.
Sometimes love is a water-filled tumbler
balanced atop an umbrella,
later it's a train emerging from a fireplace
full of your heart's smoldering embers.
If the earth is blue like an orange,
love is an invisible cloak embossed
with aubergine apples and ochre hydrangeas,
or whatever else the moment demands.

# Visiting the Black Virgin of Montserrat

The pilgrimage is not so difficult today:
Metro to train to cable car, not even two hours,
and we are 4000 feet high. No clouds today.
For lunch we have bread and wine and ham.

Just after the noon Mass, we begin to queue,
a line of the faithful and the merely interested.
In front of me, a woman wears a tight, snow-
leopard-print mini dress and red stilettos.
Her heels click a steady cadence.
Her husband is ignoring her.
Her language is eastern European.
She has traveled far.
By the time we reach the Virgin,
the woman is weeping.

Before we descend from the mountain,
I stop to buy heather-scented honey
that I will smuggle through customs
wedged deep inside a packed shoe.

## Model in Dior Suit, Walking Poodles in Paris

after photograph by Louise Dahl-Wolfe

If it weren't for the other woman
between you and the Eiffel Tower
I couldn't believe any of this—
Perfection is a strong word,
but there you are, right foot
slightly pitched forward
(an illusion of motion?)
one poodle, black, echoes
with raised front left paw,
seems still just a puppy,
the other dog, darker, bigger,
more like the tower, fixed;
together they are bookends on leashes,
one attentive, the other moving
away from you, everything reflected
in wet pavement. But why grasp
a riding crop in your gloved right hand?
Isn't the tilt of your hat, your poise,
enough for this exercise? You are
smiling; the other woman is not.
She is older, no dogs, no hat,
just the element that constructs
the distant truth of you.

# But for the Grace

*Always for the first time*
*I hardly know you by sight*
—A. Breton

The bells of the Sorbonne just chimed 3:00.
I am clothed only
in shadows from window-box geraniums
and my wedding ring.

You are snoring your wine sleep sounds—
long inspirations, punctuated
by occasional gasps—
such breathlessness once frightened me.

Being alone in Paris frightened me.

Being alone frightened me.

Perhaps it is this fear
that beckoned me tonight,
compelled me to watch over,
to pray for, the staggering drunk below
who bawls curses to the air
because he isn't sure
he will find his way home.

# Settling Down

We are on a beach in Tarragona, Spain. It's a Friday afternoon in June. The sun slips in and out of the white clouds. I almost need a sweater. We have changed into our swimsuits here in the open. We could just as well be naked. The wind and sand are blasting our skin. I cannot stop squinting. The water feels like the blue color it is. You bounce to warm yourself and look giddy in the photo I take. You are giddy. So am I. There is no one to take a photo of us together. I bury my face in the hollow near your left shoulder. In less than an hour we will be forced to pack it in. How can I say this without it being a love poem? Months from now, sand will spill from the totebag's pocket onto our bedroom floor in Atlanta—the grains settling quickly between the planks.

# Encountering Mary Outside Lourdes

On the road leaving Lourdes
near the shuttered *Discothèque My Sweet Lord,*
stands another ubiquitous statue
of the Blessed Virgin Mary:
*Our Lady of the Corn Stalks,*
I'm calling her. Nothing here
is an apparition. This is Mary
in the everyday, the ordinary,
the kind of woman who might
stop you in the parking lot
as you are leaving the local *salon de thé,*
crumbs of a croissant still on your lips,
to say your tunic *est très jolie,*
that *les couleurs sont bonnes pour vous,*
then realizing you don't speak much French,
gently runs her thumb down
the middle of your body, like a surgeon
about to do a heart bypass, then
outlines your figure with both hands a bit wider
than you are, and says something
about *les boutons* as she scissors with fingers.
For a moment she stares intently into to your eyes,
waits for some kind of recognition. Not knowing
what to say or how to say it, you can only nod.
She waves as she drives away in her Citroën.
This is a woman who knows everything about alteration.

## Summer Slumber

No sleep is like a summer sleep,
long days before air-conditioning,
naps were the only thing worth any energy.
On top of great-granny's faded blue,
popcorn-pattern chenille bedspread,
I dreamed I could fly.

In my twenties, I would retreat
upstairs in a hundred-year-old
North Georgia farmhouse, Saturday afternoons,
when even reading became too exhausting.
I would switch the box fan on high, place it
at the foot of a bed that sunk low in the middle.
Fitfully, I dreamed of trains.

In three days, I will turn forty-eight.
The 17ᵗʰ C. *Maison Vieilhescazes*,
its cool red tiles no match for the July sun,
is a French respite from my work-a-day world.
This first afternoon, I find myself slipping
back to the past, into a sweet, summer slumber,
in a present where I dream only of sleep.

# The Sounds of Silence

In the studio this morning,
I have closed my eyes,
taken the time to listen.
John is cutting the back lawn,
the warble of the mower
is punctuated by birdsong.
The wind is rattling the shutters.
Another studio door opens,
footsteps patter toward
the wash sink, a rush of water
splashes into the ceramic basin,
then steps retrace themselves.
A door latch snaps closed.
A woman's voice drifts up
from the street out front.
There's the sound of glass
clanking in the village recycling bin.
In the distance I hear a truck
shifting gears, huffing, as it
passes over the Garonne bridge.

You are out looking for
inspiration in the countryside
in the rental car the agent warned us
was *silent*. He meant hybrid,
but couldn't translate that.
Silence is often what I long for,
in a place without interruption,
but that doesn't really translate either.

# Crowning Glory

The small chapel, once
a private family retreat,
where the household women
could remain hidden from view,
is alive with artists today.

On the altar, two seamstresses
are arranging wigs, feathered masks,
and Marie Antoinette style gowns
alongside reworked party fashions.

The featured mannequin, midriff bare,
black damask cocktail dress and fishnets,
is all the more striking because of
the Renee Russo *Thomas Crowne Affair* style wig.

Hair is a precious thing.

In the military, recruits had
their heads shaved to eliminate
any sense of individuality.
When women joined the ranks,
the barbers stepped aside.

Some orthodox women
shave their heads after marriage
or cover their hair in public
or never cut their hair,
in line with whatever version of
proper womanhood they adhere.

I've had friends, cancer attacking
breasts and uteruses and ovaries,
lose all their hair,
the chemotherapy erasing
more than mutated cells.

A transvestite friend worries
most about his hair,
the wigs key to any convincing
version of womanhood.

Every six weeks, I visit the salon,
have the stylist reset the hair clock
to younger, auburn days.

Marie Antoinette was separated
from her head and from her hair:
the Revolution demanded
two deaths at once.

# Our Hands

Last night at the *théâtre en balade*,
the cashier helped her young son
stamp our hands with a red ink logo
to show we had paid the price of admission.

You snapped a photo of our hands
before the *théâtre en balade*
as we walked along the Garonne:
red ink logos and black jet rings.

Two lovers who almost didn't find each other,
the photo you snapped proves
how easily my hand fits inside yours
as we kiss beside the Garonne.

We promenade with the townspeople,
two lovers lost in the evening's merriment.
As the *histoire de la ville* unfolds,
my hand rests easily in yours.

The cashier nudges her son along,
as we promenade with the townspeople.
We have paid the price of admission:
Our story is only beginning to unfold.

# Rifts

Just off the abbey square
our dessert has arrived:
a soft meringue
and apricot cream canyon,
filled with a rivulet
of lavender oil, effluvial
on a thin, white plate.

We are listening
to the Sunday carillon recital.
"I think it's Bach," you say,
but I hear only indiscriminate
bells, and an infant, unseen,
wailing nearby. I suspect
he is teething—enamel tearing
through swollen gum, his
drool trickling onto cobblestone.

# Landscape

We are four courses into the tasting menu when the cheese trolley arrives at L'Auberge de Bardigues. The mosaic of milk, a couple of pyramids among partial wheels in creamy whites punctuated by the occasional flash of green, blue, and gray, is a tale of the local landscape. One of the village cats (mottled in the same colors) jumps onto the limestone wall surrounding the terrace. Our waitress wanders down the road with a tray of drinks for a group of men playing *pétanque*. It is nearly midnight. I feel your leg brush against mine. On our way here, we pulled the car off the road by a field of sunflowers. Van Gogh was not hyperbolic—ochre waves undulate for miles. I stood on the edge of the field, the tail of my black linen dress flirted with the stalks. For a moment, I felt as if I could let those cyclopes engulf me, but, with the snap of your camera, I was captured again.

# The Broken Mirror

The moment it hit the tile,
I could feel my soul slip a little,
not leave me, just shift
like a tectonic plate, somewhere deep
where no one goes.

After consulting the online oracles
I threw salt over my shoulder,
spun counterclockwise three times,
enough to make me dizzy.
Bad luck right there.

I have saved a jagged piece.
Tomorrow I will take the #14 bus
to Poblenou; in view of the stone angels
I will touch the shard to a tombstone—
leave this part of my fate in Spain.

# Local Legends

For Christine McAllister

Mrs. M. knew a white witch, apropos
and fortunate since her Burmese friend
refused to revisit the Auvillar abode
convinced it was haunted. She needed amends
for an old ghost, some form of recompense,
to make him go politely, relocate
perhaps just up the hill to a ruined manse
where he'd disturb no one, no matter how late.
At the appointed hour, palm frond in hand
Mrs. M. recited the gobbledygook,
transcribed for her by the witch in England,
insisted her house was no place for spooks.
Such are the tales you hear in tiny, French towns,
especially from Englishmen (or women) who might be around.

# Market Day

Words like *fraise* and *fromage* fill the air,
conversations rapidly swirl around me.
I understand almost nothing,
until I round a corner to the familiar—
the scene, unmistakable,
proof that women everywhere
make the same jokes, play the same games.
Either of these women could have
been my grandmother, giggling the way
only old women can: *"Voila!"* exclaims one
as she dons an extravagant straw hat,
cocks her head to the left, bats her eyes.
*"Ooh la la,"* the other answers,
as she fans the tail of the cotton shift
clinging to her legs in the July heat.
Back and forth they go.
The young man working the stall
stands patiently, yet attentively,
knows enough to say nothing:
acceptance, a woman's prerogative.

# To the Roses of Auvillar

### 1: Ronsard Pinks

Grandmothers interlocking thorny arms, heavy
from the weight of old beauty.
They could tumble, but hold each other
steady with omniscience,
overhang cobbled walls,
watch our every step.

### 2: White

Hint of dull jade in your complexion,
the never-married cousin of the Garonne—
easily overlooked
behind the garrulous fuchsia.
Village cats brush their heads against you,
and other people's children
clutch you to their chests before Sunday dinner.

### 3: Red

Being the pretty sister is never easy:
everyone wants you at their table,
expects splendor and grace,
feels free to embrace you,
take in your fragrance—
abandons you the moment
you deign to wither a mote.

*4: Yellow*

The baby sister, you cannot decide
what you want to be, think yourself
already grown, more sunflower than rose.
You dance in river wind on lanky legs,
your petals always tousled,
wait for someone to take you away.

# When the Dog Bites…

Okay, so it didn't really bite me
this angry bit of French white fluff,
the terrier I'm now calling "Claw,"
that attacked me like I was a Norman
intent on invading the village. Instead
I was simply climbing *Rue St. Catherine*
a short, but steep distance, my only
pilgrimage along the *Camino de Santiago*.

In 1204, the port still full of boatmen,
this was the rough part of town
where the brothel harlots, no doubt,
had many scars worse than the one
I will have on my left calf.

Poets are supposed to understand pain,
retell it in ways that make it beautiful,
but mine is a trivial, albeit ugly, wound
that merely kept me from my dinner.

## Surveillances

Last night a spider
wove her web across the black
leatherette desk chair.

*

The village rooster
is a madman this noontime:
He breeds only scorn.

*

Cigarette smoke drifts
like bereavement through window:
Perched sparrow departs.

*

It may rain today,
or it may not rain today:
Only the wind knows.

*

Little girl on bike
persistent at garden gate:
she will not dismount.

*

Dove coos under eaves.
Bull frogs croak by the river.
Amalgamation.

*

Flowers are silent?
Have you seen the hydrangeas?
Purple explosion!

*

A pilgrim passes.
his donkey follows closely.
So much devotion.

*

Neglected door hinge
sounds like a mournful cello
when the wind plays it.

## Petals on a Wet, Black Bough

Always there is *the one*:
often it is a child, jumping
or dancing or squealing or waving
with joyous, juvenile madness;
or a young woman so stricken
with a particular grief
that she is indifferent to
her public spectacle, unconcerned
by what any of us might think;
or it is the menacing one,
whose difference is manifest
in an unsettling, direct gaze,
an unwelcome connection,
and no matter how many
people are crammed in between,
you experience the vulnerability
that only strangers can feel
in a crowd.

# Flight

The flash of color, green sometimes blue,
swooshes from tree to tree, and you find
it hard to convince yourself that you've seen anything.

Away from the busy streets, a colony of monk parakeets
dazzle amid the laden orange trees at Pedralbes Monastery:
in this place belief comes easy.

Mornings, if you walk up Passeig de Gràcia, the windows
of grand Modernisme apartments thrown open wide,
you imagine the flutter of escaping wings—

you almost see the ghost of a grandmother, scanning the skies,
cursing sons and daughters and grandchildren who lacked devotion,
who left the cage door open when she died.

In the shadow of Tibidabo, where tradition holds the devil
told Jesus all these things could be his
(the mountains, the sea, these beautiful birds),

I recite a prayer of hope, knowing that once I am gone
it will be hard to believe in what I cannot see.

# Writing Poetry is a Luxury

*And she lets the river answer.*
—Leonard Cohen

The Garonne has no time
to speak to me,
a turbulent mix,
its tidal bore
menacing,
pushes me away
from the water's edge—
just another half-sunk barge
run aground,
just another bit of
entangled driftwood.

Even the frogs mock me,
growl and chirp
warnings
to keep my distance,
silent only
when I retreat.

From the opposite bank,
a church bell chimes 11:00,
in Auvillar
the bells toll twice.
A reminder
not to miss something?

The current is swift.
I am trying to write a poem.

The river will not answer me.

The river only speaks French.

# THE NEW WORLD

# Rereading Gary Snyder's "On Top"

*turn it inside out*

All this old stuff goes underneath
wedge it here   pack it there
set a fire          and wait.
Into the brightest embers
blow a steady breath,
ignite a piece of paper, let it burn,
now.
Watch it smolder.

Inspiration like faint smoke.

# Always Open

In the dream, I'm back on the road
driving south from Lincoln, NE
toward Kansas City, windows half way
down, Midwest winter air smacking me
awake, reminding me to breathe.
I'm suffering.
Homesickness is the story
I tell, but I know there's more to it,
this loneliness, these too fast
heartbeats, this need to escape.

Just outside St. Joe, traffic
from the KC aiport roars
overhead, and just off the exit
I see it, glowing warm yellow
in the darkness, so I pull in.
This is no photoshopped Hopper
*Nighthawks.* No, this is home,
always open, always there
waiting for me past any curfew.

I shake snow from my hair,
find the place empty, except for
one counter stool, which begins
to spin and Bourdain tells me to
join him, so I do because
I've got nowhere else to be.
I shout, "Scattered, smothered,
covered, diced, and capped,"
and laughter erupts. Now the place
is full of people I couldn't save.
We are all eating pecan waffles,
telling each other stories, and I say,

"Someday, maybe, I'll find a way to be happy,"
and Bourdain says, "Don't you have
somewhere you should be?"
The faint sound of the airplanes
begins to amplify, everything begins to shake.
I dive down, cover my ears,
shut my eyes to the looming shadows—

startled, I find myself back in Atlanta,
you are snoring again,
and, for once, for always, this makes me happy.

## Tending the Sick

Because I was feeling poorly,
you stopped at the grocery
to pick up spinach and roses,

and as I slumped at the table,
my pajama sleeve steeped
in a bowl of chicken stew,

you apologized for not remembering
the grapes, which confused me,
so, you kissed the top of my head,

and explained: in England, it is always
grapes and flowers for the sick.

# Living in an old flower shop

is not the most eccentric thing
I've ever done,
not really even a conscious choice
just the sort of happenstance
poverty sometimes offers.

I was twenty-two, worked three jobs,
but on Sunday afternoons
could walk a quarter mile
down a gravel road
to visit my grandparents,
sit on their porch, drink sweet tea,
eat Little Debbie oatmeal pies.

The *poet me* wants to turn all this
into metaphor, some
exceptional conceit,
but I don't remember much
about those two years,
just the empty cooler turned closet,
the broken bedroom window that sliced
my right palm from pinky to thumb,
and nightmares of chrysanthemums.

# Proximity

The young possum foraging
outside my office window
seems unconcerned by my presence—
after all, I am the one who's trapped.
I snack on almonds, watch
it nibble whatever it can find,
and though I am inclined to share,
I know that opening the window
will change the world.

# In My Kitchen in Atlanta

for Allen Ginsberg

You do like to surprise.
So, the mornings I stumble
into the kitchen,
unprepared even to put on
the kettle, much less
face the day, only to discover
your naked body, contorting
in what you swear are Tai Chi moves,
I grapple with your eccentricities
which push beyond the surreal,
beyond the sublime,
beyond what anyone should submit
to before the sun rises.
This I could live with, Allen.
But when you begin to lose focus,
criticize my bathrobe,
scold me for eating bacon,
mock me for not writing
something important each day,
I want to tell you to take it up
with the universe—except
I know you will,
and, ultimately, I'll read some line
you wrote years before my birth
and I will feel the reproach
meant for those you knew
would be inclined to listen.
Nevertheless, you are always welcome here.
Try not to step on the cats.

# Mapplethorpe: Early Polaroids

### 1.   *Clarissa Dalrymple, 1973/75*

If some native tribes are right
to believe that a photograph steals
your soul, this portrait
is evidence you might
have offered yours freely.
You look perfect, and I say this
without ever having met you,
without having ever heard your name.
How much did you relinquish
when the camera captured you?

### 2:   *Untitled, 1973*

It is just a still life—
white table model, rotary dial,
phone number almost legible,
the folds of a damasked curtain,
maybe gold or green,
brushing against the countertop.
The short corkscrew cable casts
a near perfect reflection across
glassy linoleum, and I expect
it to ring any moment,
but have no idea how to answer.

### 3.   *Untitled (Manfred), 1974*

Yeah, so he's naked.
You probably expected that before
you walked into the gallery;
that's not the point.
When the armpit is more
conspicuous than the penis,
you should question your expectations
there is so much more for us
fixed in 5 inches square,
something we attempt to remember
from a moment that was never our own.

## Nimbus

When evening rain comes,
as it often does this time of year,
I am reminded of you.
Strange, because it was not raining
the night you died.
It was warm for February.
We held hands. I switched off
the lights. It was very dark—

unlike in that portrait,
the one I did not inherit,
you on Cape Cod watching something,
probably your children playing in the water.
You shield your eyes, and it is impossible
to tell whether the sun is rising or setting.
I never got around to asking you about it.

The painting is awash in amber, ochre, flax.
The light envelops you.
You have your back to me.

## The Other Side of the Tracks

What if I chucked it all,
began calling myself Candi,
(with a heart over the "i")
stopped in at Wal-Mart to buy
a jean-skirt, a tank top,
and a can of Aqua Net,
hitchhiked to a small town
just outside Birmingham, AL
taking on a part-time waitress gig,
mornings at the Waffle House,
evenings spent pot-smoking
and fucking anyone who could pay
enough, just to make ends meet,
dealt a little meth near train crossings
from a junker with a hood that would pop up
whenever I gunned the engine or drove over 45,
until the day came when I saw
a Laura Ashley knockoff jumper
hanging out of the Salvation Army bin
and felt the Spirit move me,
took to preaching from the self-serve pumps
at the Shell station that sells trucker porn,
answering to any Biblical name,
believing, like proper church matrons,
that I was somehow more redeemable,
worth a dollar's charity, when before
they couldn't be bothered to leave
me a tip when I served them coffee.

# What Loneliness Looks Like

From my hotel window the reflection
of my body is superimposed on the outline
of rock that appears closer than it is,
a jagged edge against the ochre evening sky,
color fading upward into darkening blue.
Lights flicker on, then pulsate,
first at the Palms, then Gold Coast, then Rio.
I sweep my eyes east along Flamingo Road
toward the Bellagio and the Strip.
Downstairs a young woman, maybe
not so young, in an ill-fitted froth of white,
stumbles, braces herself against a slot machine.
A man in a powder blue tuxedo arrives,
hands her a cocktail larger than the bouquet
she tosses across her shoulder to no one.
On my flight here, I took a photo of Hoover Dam
with its white towers, silent guards.
A long drought has left less to hold back.

# A Plague of Acorns

for Steve Lewis

This morning I startled awake:
the plonk and rattle on the roof,
and then the skittering
squirrels clawing after
what summer had dropped.

On the porch, I sipped my tea,
the morning air chilly
for the first time in months,
and all around me, petunias
and begonias gone scraggly,
ringed by flung out soil,
acorns half-buried, a hole in every pot.
Those seeds will only rot.

Monday traffic is mad.
A young squirrel dodges cars
coming, fast, in both directions—
his luck finally runs out.
At a stoplight, I glance in the mirror,
notice another year of lines
etched along my mouth and eyes,
when you burst into memory,
still young, still smiling, but still.
It is September 13th.
Fourteen years have passed.

On the first anniversary I wrote about loss,
mentioned your answering machine,
the make of your gun,
but now the only thing that matters,
the only thing that remains,
is the hole you left, where nothing grows.

## Listening to Michelle Obama Denounce Donald Trump's Abuse of Women

Mid-October, work conference in Denver
I'm just finishing one of those "free"
breakfasts at a Hampton Inn
served up on small round, too low tables
topped with cell phones and room keycards,
thankful that the TV is set
to CNN and not FOX. Thankful,
that is, until the man sitting next to me
says to his friend, "Why does she always
have to raise her voice, be so angry?"
Every woman around me shifts in her seat—
except one. She is native American.
This is *her* country. She says loudly
to her bouncer-looking husband,
"Go get me another biscuit."

Something buried deep beneath
my whiteness, maybe ancient marrow
within the Cherokee cheekbones I inherited
from great, great grandmother, Hester,
begins to leach out, surface.
Jostling his table, his hot coffee,
isn't hard with my woman's hips—
revolutions begin this way.

# On Being the Only of My Circle
## Not to Watch *Twin Peaks*

Laura Palmer's death did not haunt me. She lurked only at the edges of my reality, no need for understanding who killed her, or why, or where—the Red Room, the Black Lodge, just places where I know someone else's evil resides.

Lynch's world, though, is familiar enough. I've accepted a turbulent ride with him down Mulholland—found myself willing to slip into whatever cloak of amnesia I could claim.

I understand what he's about.

Truth is, most of my friends, feet singed by bright-hot, blue television rays, were eager to share the heat, to tell the tale, over and again—everything I needed to learn about *Twin Peaks*, swallowed past a lump in my throat, with tequila and slices of cherry pie.

All of us, most of our waking lives, dreamlike, are trying to keep a parallel distance—because the *real* is always more surreal than the *imagined*—because some beautiful child is always dead, begging for us to hear her story.

# New

The teller dropped the coin.
It bounced twice, and spun
on edge for a few seconds
before it fluttered flat in front of me—
a tiny shock of brilliance.

Somewhere I imagined a boy
shaking a tamborine,
a belly dancer, her hip-scarf
jiggling rows of fake coins.
I felt the phantom impression
of the penny I placed
in my sequined wedding shoe last May,
and silently I made a wish.

Near the exit a hazel-eyed girl,
waiting for her father,
waved a fairy's wand, and spun
like a ballerina on a music box.
Some wishes should be shared—
I put the shiny charm in her palm.

# Marriage Parable

Our bellhop cautions:
the honeymoon suite's fireplace
is on a timer.

# Age of Aquarius 2.0

Stop by Starbuck's and grab a to-go cup,
your boss at the software company
might forgive tardiness if you arrive
bearing a soy latte and two multi-grain scones.
Head for the subway,
cue up Joni Mitchell on your iPhone.
You heard about her in that movie,
the one about the lesbian parents,
and from Emma Thompson in *Love Actually*:
"I love her. And true love lasts a lifetime."
You snag your Free People paisley tunic
(the one that cost a week's pay)
as you negotiate the revolving door,
your five-inch Manolos hold you up, just,
as you toss an air-kiss toward a passing colleague.
After work, join friends at a local bar,
drink cocktails from champagne saucers
rinsed with nouveau absinthe, and think
about dancing. You almost twirl your way
toward the guy in the Warby Parker tortoise-shells,
notice, just in time, his boyfriend arriving.
You wish you had a boyfriend, someone to love
for an age, or for tonight.

## The Necklace

When I was a two,
yes, the terrible year,
most days my mother
wore a thin belt
draped across her shoulders
a leather necklace, a warning.
She could snap it like a whip
with the same speed
that I could pull out
dresser drawers to climb.
She was trying to cope
with my sense of adventure.
One day, she left it off,
and I tipped over my piggy bank.
When it hit the floor, a shard
nearly missed my left eye,
instead tore a jagged opening
into the bridge of my nose.
Her choice of jewelry
may seem cruel to some,
but it is because she fashioned
her threat so materially,
that I learned
to make more careful choices.

## Walking in the Northeast Georgia Mountains
## Just Before My Fiftieth Birthday

Maybe I'm just tapping into my inner Wendell Berry, James Dickey, or Bill Stafford, but nature sure can be hard to ignore. Case in point, this morning on my walk to the creek falls at Patterson Gap, I came across a raccoon. He seemed to be taking a nap, or maybe recuperating from a wild night out with the boys. He had the look of some guys I've slept with: cute, but disheveled, the beginning of a gut peeking out between jeans and flannel shirt, skin-scent of charcoal burnt ribs mixed with Polo cologne, and a penchant for leaning against cars, trees, and riding lawnmowers. I could imagine him drinking a PBR. I kept my distance even though he seemed harmless enough. On the way back, I couldn't help myself, nudged a little closer, saw black flies buzzing a halo over him. The driver who hit this little guy probably never saw him, or maybe it was a blatant hit and run. Hard to say. Barney (because at this point he had to have a name, right?), yes, Barney's tail, atop a dewy bed of thistle, was majestic, which put me in mind of one of my earliest boyfriends who wore a coon-tail keychain on his right back belt loop. Sometimes you just know things aren't right, but it may take you years to figure out why.

## Winogrand, Untitled

The scene has enough dimensions
to draw you into the bar,
maybe late 60's, early 70's,
it only matters that you are not
in the 21st century anymore.

The man sitting along the wall
looks directly at you as if to say,
"You don't belong here,"
and you want to interrupt
the two women talking,
touch the nearest one's shoulder,
ask her where you are.

The reflection you thought
was from a flashbulb
is just a small spotlight
illuminating a place
you could easily occupy,
except the man at the end of bar
seems like he'd try to buy you a drink,
if only the bartender was around,
and then want to slide
his hand up your thigh.

You begin to catch piano notes,
eyes darting, you dizzily follow
the lines of light fixtures
until you have no idea where
you are supposed to look,
so, you reach back
for the photographer's hand—
fall back outside the frame.

# Cleaning Out the Pantry

New Year's Day, 2009

It begins when I decide
to pull the vanilla-bean-pod
from the sugar bowl
as I am sweetening
my morning cup of tea.

Today I return to the earth
what I have taken,
but have not used.
As sunlight edges the horizon,
cuts into the mist,
I sow *grains of paradise*
near the rose bush,
scatter *thyme* on oak tree roots,
sweep *allspice* under the porch.

*Parisian Bonnes Herbes,*
*Chinese Five-Spice,*
*Madras Curry,*
*Hungarian Paprika*:
these I swirl around me
(good luck for travel).
The neighborhood cats,
suspicious of my shabby robe,
judge my unkempt hair.
Mine is a cold but colorful ceremony,
each glass jar tapped empty,
then a quick puff of warm breath
to shake loose the dregs.

Finally, wanting
to hold something
of sunsets past—
The saffron I keep.

# EPILOGUE

# What We Missed

The giddy flush of young love,
we've only glimpsed a few times—
that evening in the museum
when you gave me a CD "mix-tape"
the likes of which I hadn't heard
in decades; that morning you met me
at the Dusseldorf train station,
bag thrown over your shoulder
arms wide, you lifted me off my feet,
swung me a quarter turn; that night
we drank Port until 2:00 am,
and danced our way home under fairy lights;
that afternoon we cuddled close
at the National Zoo, held your camera
at arm's length and snapped happiness.

Each morning when you bring me tea
I concede finding each other late was for the best.
Still, sometimes I mourn the years we never had
even the ones that would have destroyed us.

Karen Head is the author of *Disrupt This!: MOOCs and the Promises of Technology* (a nonfiction book about issues in contemporary higher education), as well as four books of poetry (*Sassing, My Paris Year, Shadow Boxes*, and *On Occasion: Four Poets, One Year*). She also co-edited the poetry anthology *Teaching as a Human Experience: An Anthology of Poetry*, and has exhibited several acclaimed digital poetry projects, including her project "Monumental" (part of Antony Gormley's *One and Other Project*) which was detailed in a *TIME* online mini-documentary. Her poetry appears in a number of national and international journals and anthologies. In 2010 she won the *Oxford International Women's Festival Poetry Prize*.

Head has held residencies at the Hambidge Center for the Creative Arts and Sciences and the Virginia Center for the Creative Arts-France. She has also taught in study abroad programs in Barcelona, Spain and Oxford, England.

She serves as Editor of the international poetry journal *Atlanta Review*, and as secretary for the Poetry Atlanta Board of Directors. On a more unusual note, she is currently the Poet Laureate of Waffle House—a title that reflects an outreach program to bring arts awareness to rural high schools in Georgia, which has been generously sponsored by the Waffle House Foundation. She is the Associate Chair and an Associate Professor in the School of Literature, Media, and Communication at the Georgia Institute of Technology, where she also serves as the Executive Director of the Naugle Communication Center. For fifteen years, Head has been a visiting artist and scholar at the Institute for American Studies at Technische Universität Dortmund in Germany.

Head grew up as an Army Brat—one reason she loves to travel so much—and has family in the Netherlands and the United Kingdom. She is a native of Atlanta, Georgia, where she lives with her very English husband, and fellow traveler, Colin Potts.

CPSIA information can be obtained
at www.ICGtesting.com
Printed in the USA
FSHW011119301020

9 781604 542554